QUARTER HORSE SPIRIT

SPIRIT OF THE HORSE SERIES

Words By Betsy Sikora Siino

BOWTIE
PRESS

Images By Bob Langrish

To my dear friend Audrey, in memory of the horses on Chief Joseph's Trail.
—B.S.S.

Nick Clemente, special consultant
Ruth Berman, editor-in-chief
Doug Kraus, designer

Library of Congress Cataloging-in-Publication Data

Siino, Betsy Sikora.
    Quarter horse spirit / words by Betsy Sikora Siino ; images by Bob
Langrish.
        p.   cm. -- (Spirit of the horse series)
    ISBN 1-889540-17-X
    1. Quarter horse.   I. Title.   II. Series.
    SF293.Q3S475   1998
    636.1'33--dc21   97-32169
                                                                  CIP

The horses in this book are referred to as *he* or *she* in alternating chapters,
unless their gender is apparent from the activity discussed.

Photographs on pages 26 and 27 are courtesy of © Charles Mann; p. 35,
© Dusty L. Perin; p. 54, (©James A. Rae) the American Quarter Horse
Association; p.55, © Sharon P. Fibelkorn

BowTie™ Press
3 Burroughs
Irvine, California 92618

Manufactured in the United States of America

First Printing May 1998

10 9 8 7 6 5 4 3 2 1

Table of Contents

The Melting Pot

One plus one equals two. Cowboy plus horse equals hero. While historians may debate the validity of this latter equation, the fact remains that within the annals of American mythology, the all-American cowboy holds a prominent position. Chalk it up to the media, chalk it up to wishful thinking, but no matter how one tries to explain it, there is no denying that the cowboy's image exerts a powerful, even comforting, influence on the American imagination.

We see this in countless little boys and girls, small felt cowboy hats perched upon their heads, wobbling in miniature western-style boots that provide the clop-clop hoofbeats of their imaginary horses. We see it in pinstriped corporate types who dream of chucking it all and, as was done in the film *City Slickers*, driving a herd of cattle across the range. And we see it in the television and movie images of Matt Dillon, Wyatt Earp, Ben Cartright, and every swaggering cowboy that John Wayne ever portrayed. When country singer Willie Nelson warbles affectionately that his heroes have always been cowboys, he touches a cultural familiarity ingrained deep within the American consciousness.

Yet while many a youngster and many a weary adult may idolize the cowboy and his much romanticized, ruggedly independent lifestyle, the cowboy couldn't have come this far had he not had a hero of his own: His horse. That horse was the American quarter horse, a legendary animal today described with pride as "America's horse."

The Melting Pot

Like the cowboy, the quarter horse is the quintessential American, his roots and his very existence spawned and fortified by the best of the melting pot of cultures and genetic material that have made America great. Yet while the image of this robust, muscular animal comes to mind the moment the word *cowboy* is uttered, the quarter horse's story did not begin on the open range of the American West, the region with which this breed is most closely associated. No, this equine pioneer's story began long before his human counterparts started to venture out into that vast western wilderness. It began almost four centuries ago, mirroring every step of the way the story of America itself.

The quarter horse, though a breed developed in America, boasts roots that, like those of many Americans themselves, were planted originally in Europe. When Spanish explorers set sail to "discover" the New World, they found that world already populated by native people, most of whom were fascinated by the horses who had accompanied the newcomers from across the ocean. As time passed, many of these animals, horses of Barb, Arabian, Turk, and Andalusian blood, found their way into the hands of Native Americans, who demonstrated an almost uncanny instinct for breeding and raising fine horses. Their skills subsequently spawned a healthy equine population that was already thriving by the time English settlers claimed the eastern coast of North America as their new home in the seventeenth century.

While a variety of Native American tribes throughout what would become the United States nurtured distinct types of horses, key to the quarter horse's story were the horses of the Chickasaw Indians of the southeastern United States. English settlers quickly recognized certain characteristics of these fine animals that could profoundly enrich their horses' English and otherwise European bloodlines. Speed, for one. European settlers had an unquenchable thirst for horse racing, and the Chickasaw horses were lightning fast. In a successful attempt to produce horses with a dedicated work ethic, the powerful physique to match, and the speed to brighten their spare leisure hours, the settlers crossed their English horses with those swift-footed Chickasaw mounts, and unknowingly forged

the foundation of what would someday become one of the most popular, most versatile breed of horse in the world.

Even more than three centuries ago, it was evident to all who knew him that the product of these early American breeding efforts, the horse who would become known as the quarter horse, had something special. Benefiting from the same brand of multicultural hybrid vigor that has marked the character of the American people themselves, he was a tireless and able worker with a well-muscled, compact build, and a gentle disposition. In other words, he was an equine dream come true.

In his early days as racehorse, the quarter horse's success at running a short course—a quarter-mile—was dependent upon his ability

to "leave the gate" and reach his top speed instantly, or, as is described in contemporary quarter horse racing circles, "explosively." Most races were weekend affairs, pitting two horses against each other in short tests of speed, often along the primitive roads of early America's quaint little towns. Those horses who excelled in supplementing their owners' incomes with their winnings—and those who proved potent in siring swift progeny such as the legendary Janus, who did so in North Carolina from 1756 to 1780—earned the exalted titles of Celebrated American Quarter Running Horses, or Famous and Celebrated Colonial Quarter Pathers. Indeed, these horses could even outrun the Thoroughbred once this breed made his grand entrance on American soil in the nineteenth century, but so would this development ultimately mark the decline of the quarter horse's colonial racing career when sprinting was overshadowed by the Thoroughbred's long-distance forte.

Never one to be rendered obsolete by circumstance or a swifter opponent, with the rise of the Thoroughbred in the 1800s the quarter horse simply moved on to a new destiny. As those early Americans began to answer the siren's song emanating beyond the western horizon, it was only natural that they would take their talented and much admired quarter horses with them. The horses again played a crucial and high-profile role in America's history, pulling wagons and buggies occupied by pioneer families and their belongings, carrying traveling preachers from

town to town in their efforts to ensure salvation would not overlook isolated settlers, and providing transportation to country doctors in the days when men of medicine still made housecalls. And in the West, like a prodigal son returning to his homeland, the quarter horse would discover his true calling. In the West, he would discover his cow sense.

So began the legendary partnership between quarter horse and cowboy. But life on the ranges of Texas, Oklahoma, Colorado, Arizona, Wyoming, Nevada, New Mexico, and the like was not quite as romantic as one might be led to believe from the story told on the movie screen. Summers in the West would swelter, prairie winds could knock a man from his horse with a single gust, winters could chill any warm-blooded creature to the

bone, and the backbreaking and unpredictable conditions of driving cattle dominated a man's time from dawn to dusk with rarely a day off to lounge around the local saloon. Through it all, the cowboy's success, and sometimes his life, depended on his bond with his horse.

There was no horse better suited to this job than those quarter-mile racers from the East. This was an animal of endurance, solid legs, and a strong back, a horse who could carry a rider all day over rugged, often treacherous terrain. He could move those "little doggies" along with agility, balance, and speed, and he could stop on a dime when it came time to "cut" a calf from the herd or foil a bull's attempt to launch a stampede. He was an easy keeper with a warm and willing disposition that made him friend as well as partner on the trail, and, if given the proper respect, he could predict his rider's next move almost before the cowboy himself even knew what that might be. Some horse. No wonder horse theft in the American West was a capital offense.

Yet throughout his celebrated past, the horse sometimes referred to as the Billy or the Steeldust, remained for the most part a horse with no name. He bred true, and his pedigree was obviously maintained carefully if not formally, but it was not until the twentieth century that America's oldest native breed was made official.

Several horses were responsible for providing the foundation of the contemporary quarter horse such as racehorse Peter McCue,

Chapter One

who from 1895 to 1923 proved to be a phenomenal sire whose progeny never failed to inherit his speed and signature quarter horse conformation. So widely disseminated were his profound gifts that his influence is still seen in the quarter horse population today. Three famed foundation sires of Peter McCue's making were Chief, Sheik, and Hickory Bill, the latter of whom would carry on the family tradition as the sire of Old Sorrel and the great-grandsire of Wimpy. Old Sorrel and Wimpy were the pride and joy of the King Ranch in Texas, founded at the turn of the twentieth century for the breeding of the world's finest stock horses, a grand mission the operation continues to pursue today.

With such exemplary horses being produced, the quarter horse's fate was finally

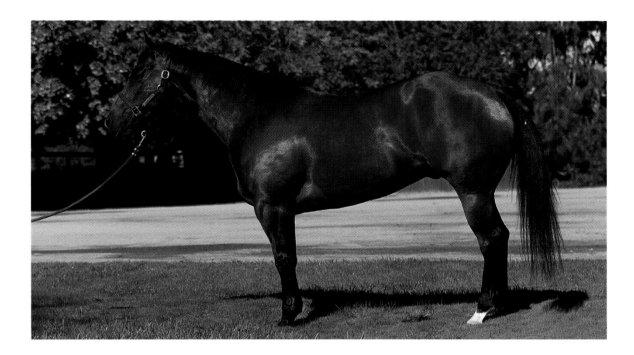

sealed in 1940 with the founding of the American Quarter Horse Association (AQHA), an organization dedicated to the registration, preservation, and promotion of the quarter horse. At last, the quarter horse had a name, the first to be registered as such being Wimpy of the King Ranch.

The founding of the AQHA ushered in a whole new era for the quarter horse, who finally had a mechanism by which his many talents could be promoted beyond the jagged cliffs and cacti of the American West. In record time, the quarter horse effortlessly recruited followers worldwide who were just naturally attracted to this very personable multitalented breed. The result? A contemporary quarter horse whose registered population throughout more than seventy countries numbers more than three million. A contemporary quarter horse who races; who participates in every English and western discipline with enthusiasm and fortitude; who works cattle; who struts his stuff in movies and television; who displays his cow sense prominently in the rodeo arena; and who, most importantly, shines as premier pleasure horse—the purest calling for a creature of such heroic proportions.

CHAPTER TWO

Horse of Many Talents

Throughout her illustrious past, the quarter horse has proven herself a diva at constantly building on her skills. Having mastered one discipline—say, one of the western classics such as reining or cutting—she moves on to the next hurdle—perhaps show jumping or dressage—always retaining her expertise in the former skill as she proceeds on to the next. The AQHA boasts "no other horses in the world are used by so many people for so many things as the American Quarter horse." At the heart of this statement is an animal, one of America's most successful exports, whose standard equipment includes a willing attitude, an intelligent head, and an astounding long-term memory. No matter what one's equine dreams, they may be granted by the quarter horse.

Horse of Many Talents

Every day, quarter horses are exploding from the gate, running those customary 440 yards at 50 miles an hour in less than 22 seconds, and claiming purses that often exceed those offered in the Thoroughbred world. Every day, quarter horses are jumping oxers in the English show-jumping arena and fallen trees on the cross-country course with grace and agility, while enjoying every moment in the air. Every day, quarter horses are rounding up cattle, predicting with clairvoyant accuracy both the cattle's actions and those of the riders on their backs. Every day, quarter horses are competing in western pleasure, competitive trail and barrel racing, exercising skills that have taken hundreds of years to hone. And every day, quarter horses are transporting their riders, riders of all ages and skill levels, along trails, city streets, and open fields in an ultimate companion partnership that has both inspired and satisfied contemporary passions for pleasure horses.

As nimble and adaptable as the nation that produced her, America's quarter horse is ever willing to tackle any and all new adventures, many of which are rooted in what were once real-life vocations for horses. Dressage, an equine ballet in which the horse's graceful moves are orchestrated via an unseen channel of communication between horse and rider, is rooted in military training traditions and the tenets of classical horsemanship. Jumping is a natural offshoot of a time when the only available means of transportation was the horse, who in turn had to do whatever was required to transport her rider over

obstacle-laden roads and trails. And the popular sport of reining, a natural vocation for the quarter horse, literally revolves around the skills and cow sense required to keep a large, potentially dangerous, herd of cattle together and moving in unison.

The instincts of which reining champions are made are passed on genetically from generation to generation of quarter horses, the newest crop of reining horses paying homage to all those who came before with each spin and rollback they are asked to execute. The tradition of riding that reining horse, of teaching her incrementally to call upon those genetic memories and anticipate the various, sometimes astounding, ballet moves required by the ten official National Reining Horse Association reining patterns, is also passed down through the generations—generations of riders. This tradition is alive and well at contemporary reining competitions, which never cease to thrill the increasingly large and enthusiastic crowds of spectators who gather to witness them.

Imagine sitting in the stands of such an event. Enter entry number 12, a slender young man in a black Stetson and tooled western boots aboard a shining chestnut quarter horse mare. Standing at the ready, the young man pats his mount's neck, smoothes her cropped mane, and whispers an affectionate word of encouragement into her delicate, attentive ears. Then, so encouraged, confident in her highly choreographed skills, the horse begins her performance. She spins right. She spins left. She circles quickly, then slows. She rolls

back. She slides to a stop. How does she not cross her legs and topple over at that dizzying speed? How does she place her feet in just the right spot at just the right second? How does she know when to perform the swift circles, when to roll back, when to slide? Her rider offers no visible signals, yet together they move as one.

And over to the side, standing thoughtfully at the fence, is an older gentleman, sharing the audience's rapt attention. His expression, however, is one not of spectator awe, but of familiar affection. The young man in the ring is his student. In painstaking detail the old man, a former reining champion himself, has shared his secrets with his younger counterpart. Respect our mare, he has told his protégé, and she will learn because it pleases

you. Armed with this fundamental understanding of the quarter horse mind, together the two men have convinced this fine animal that they understand her unique view of the world as they ask her to perform each new step in this intricate ballet. The mare in turn responds with trust and courage and a phenomenal athletic ability that suggests she certainly must have been a reining quarter horse in a previous life, as well.

And now, at the conclusion of this ultimate test of their combined efforts, the older man watches with pride as his student and his mare reap top honors. Having accepted their accolades, the two approach the mare whose skills they have nurtured with such precision. The men stroke her neck and tickle her ears. There is none better, they tell her, but that is of no concern to this horse. The admiration and respect of these men are her reward. Indeed that is all the reward the quarter horse has ever wanted. The old man knows this, of course. That is the secret. He smiles. The torch has been passed. The tradition will continue.

A Signature Profile

ome to the quarter horse is wherever his work is. Armed with a work ethic that gives new meaning to the phrase, the quarter horse is at home in any setting, at any job. For most self-respecting quarter horses, work is play especially when that work is in partnership with a trusted human, whether that be in the show ring, on the trail, or simply sharing those special moments around the barn, enjoying the ministrations of the daily grooming routine.

Yet catch a glimpse of a quarter horse at rest, sans saddle, perhaps at pasture or standing quietly by the tack shed, and what an unforgettable vision he presents. There is no mistaking the signature stock horse conformation of the classic quarter horse for any other breed.

Chapter Three

With a compact build that typically averages 15 to 16 hands, the quarter horse is a portrait of muscle in ideal equine proportion. The engine that has for centuries propelled this agile animal forward so explosively, and has thus ensured his success as champion sprinter, jumper, barrel racer, and reining horse, is the quarter horse's hindquarters—broad, round, and packed with power. Balancing out the rear is a front highlighted by a deep chest and sloping shoulders, as well as solid legs and feet, a compact back, and short cannons, all engineered genetically for sound overall structure and strength.

The quarter horse's head and neck also contribute to the unique vision that is this animal. His handsome head—characterized by a short muzzle; a broad forehead; large nostrils; bright, wide-set, intelligent eyes; and small, alert ears—typically sits at a 45-degree angle on the horse's muscular, slightly arched neck. The resulting effect is the appearance of a strong, well-defined jaw providing an ample airway that ensures the maximum ration of oxygen reaches this athlete's lungs with every breath.

Rounding out this portrait is color. The AQHA recognizes thirteen solid colors and their variations (though most quarter horses are chestnut or sorrel), with limited white markings allowed on the legs and face. Not recognized by the AQHA are quarter horses of spotted paint, pinto, and Appaloosa patterns. Quarter horses so patterned are popular nonetheless, and enjoy a devoted following of breeders and owners who register their spot-

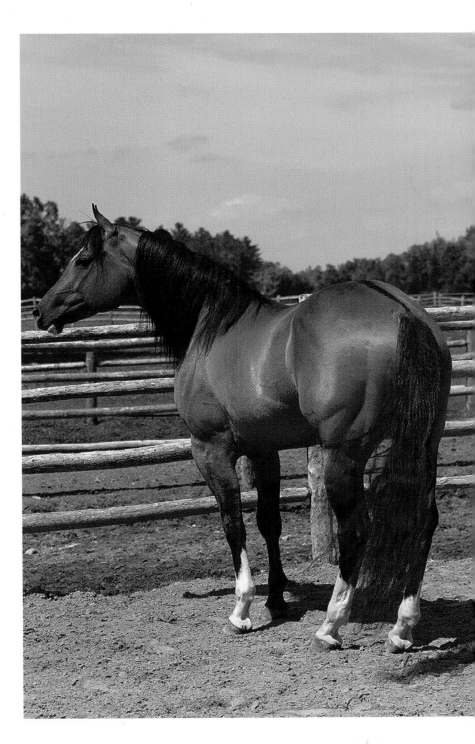

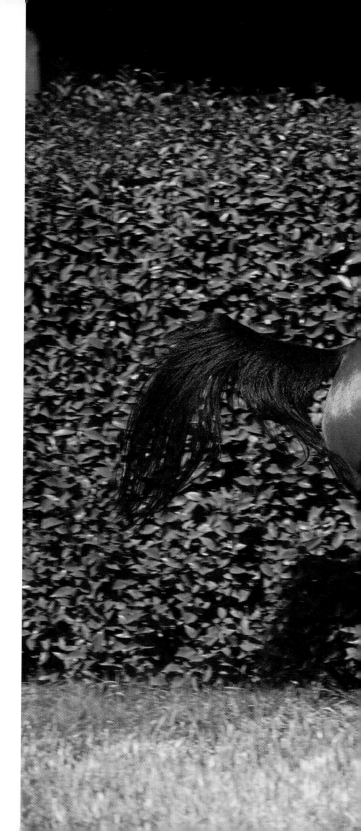

ted quarter horses with the very large and active associations that register horses of color.

The quarter horse's signature physique, the sight of which brings a wave of warmth and comfort to those who so adore this breed, has become just as recognizable throughout the world as the quarter horse name itself. In fact, even those who hardly fancy themselves horse experts can often recognize a quarter horse when they see one. A simple trip to a toy store can serve as the introductory experience. As one of the most popular breeds represented among the famous Breyer line of model horses, miniature plastic quarter horses inspired by full-size quarter horses can be seen displayed prominently in toy stores throughout the world. Available in all colors and sizes, these small sculptures have long delighted collectors of all ages and have enjoyed most-favored-toy status among generations of horse-crazed young girls.

Also familiar with this breed are film buffs and television viewers who have seen the quarter horse featured in just about every movie and television western ever made. The customary widespread admiration for the breed occurred within this context when audiences fell in love with, then mourned, Cisco (as portrayed by quarter horse Plain Justin Bar), the beloved equine companion of John Dunbar (as portrayed by Kevin Costner) in the classic epic *Dances with Wolves*. Former quarter horse racehorse Docs Keepin Time carried on this tradition with his title performance in the 1994 remake of the heart-

Chapter Three

breaking story of Black Beauty. Although the literary Beauty was no quarter horse, any casting director would be hard pressed to come up with an equine actor better suited to such a complex role.

Yet despite his success as supermodel and movie star, the most prevalent image of the quarter horse is found in far more humble settings. This is the image of the companion quarter horse, the plain old regular quarter horse, the quintessential pet quarter horse, who has for centuries stolen the hearts of human beings of all ages, races, nationalities, equestrian abilities, and bank accounts.

First and foremost, the quarter horse is a people horse. In pastures, stalls, and paddocks from one hemisphere of the planet to the other, stocky, well-muscled quarter horses of gray, chestnut, buckskin, and bay look up from their hay with kind, intelligent eyes to welcome the arrival of the people they trust most, the people they regard as family. One look at the quarter horse's familiar physique, one meeting of the eyes, and horse lovers who have had the honor of being considered family by such an animal, know in just that single magical moment of interspecies communion that they are home.

The First Year

*E*leven months have passed since that day. Eleven months ago, she looked up from her leisurely munching of sweet spring pasture grass, startled by the rattle of a truck on the gravel in the drive. An unfamiliar, though enticing, scent filled the air. Her curiosity aroused, she felt oddly drawn to the trailer that followed the truck across the rocky ground.

He backed out of the trailer, enthusiastic yet cooperative. A strapping stallion, he was ideal in every way: 15.3 hands, a shining sorrel coat, all the right muscles in all the right places. His résumé, too, was in order: championship marks in western pleasure, hunt seat, and dressage. His track record as stud was impressive as well, his offspring proving to take after Dad in all athletic endeavor. His newest prospective mate's interest, however, was rooted not in evaluations of his conformation or career, but in a far more primitive call. The matchmakers had chosen well. This mare, of equal quality in both physique and talent, had been chosen as vessel to carry on four hundred years of genetic tradition. Called to this grand venture, together she and this fine stallion would create a foal who would combine the best of their breed's heritage in a single dynamic package.

And now, at last, after eleven months of waiting, top-notch prenatal care, and optimum nutrition, the foal arrives. A filly. Her obvious resemblance to her mother is a cause for celebration. From the warmth and security of Mom's womb, she is thrust wet and clumsy and confused onto a bed of clean

straw. Yet even at just minutes of age, she acknowledges an inner voice. *Stand*, it tells her, as it has told her kind for tens of thousands of years at this crucial moment. The straw is soft and fragrant, but she knows she must obey. She gathers her slender, still-damp legs beneath her, and, with a burst of exhausted energy, she pushes upward. She remains prone. She tries, tries again—she is, after all, a quarter horse. Finally, she is victorious. There will be many such efforts and many such victories in her future.

She stands wobbling on legs that are foal spindly, yes, but not as spindly as one expects of a foal just a few tender minutes old. Even her rump seems a bit meatier, a bit rounder than those of most newborns. And within her

Chapter Four

eyes, eyes that have thus far viewed only a bed of straw, the wooden panels of a dimly lit stall, and the lovely chestnut animal who stands beside her to whom she is instinctively drawn, is a lively expression that suggests she has begun what promises to be a grand adventure within this strange new place in which she has found herself.

Soon within the filly's newfound field of vision appears an odd, two-legged creature. She approaches quietly. She makes soft, soothing sounds. She strokes the filly's broad forehead and moves her hands gently down the youngster's neck, her shoulders, her well-sculpted legs. The unspoken message within her soft touch convinces the filly to trust her. The stranger seems to understand this. Slowly she picks up an unusual object, the configura-

The First Year 47

tion of straps that is the foal halter, and places it gently on the youngster's head. Sure, Mom is number one in the foal's esteem, but this two-legged being and her soothing ways, designed to help the foal bond to a worthy member of the human species, isn't so bad herself.

In the days that follow, the filly's initial suspicions about the adventurous nature of this place prove to be correct. Given her open quarter horse mind and the heritage that has produced it, she embraces each new experience with wonder. She soon discovers that more horses reside beyond the barn doors— and more people, more textures, more sounds, more sensations, more vistas within the lovely green pasture in which she spends many playful hours with Mom. Her involvement with her world will grow ever more intimate as she learns not only to accept new sites and experiences as part of the landscape but to discover her own role within them, as well.

Sometime between her fourth and sixth month of life, our young filly, now skilled at walking cooperatively at the end of a lead rope, well accustomed to the presence of other horses in her midst, and more brazen in her independent forays away from Mom's side, will learn that she need no longer rely on her mother's milk for sustenance. It may be a difficult lesson, hard on both her and her dam, but the precocious youngster will soon find herself occupied instead by other pursuits. Savvy as they are about the quarter horse mind, her human handlers will spend many hours grooming her; exposing her to new, exciting, though potentially spooky, sights, sounds, and environments; and perhaps even presenting her, like a debutante, in the halter class show ring.

Nevertheless, it will be many months before this filly feels the weight of a saddle on her back, let alone that of a rider, but she will excel at the preliminary exercises that will prepare her for that fateful moment. Given her breed, the process will come naturally to her. As she matures, she will greet each of the many new challenges sent her way not with fear or suspicion, but with the same coolheaded, wide-eyed sense of adventure that marked her first moments of life within that quiet, clean stall. One would expect nothing less from a quarter horse. It's in the genes.

CHAPTER FIVE

Show of Shows

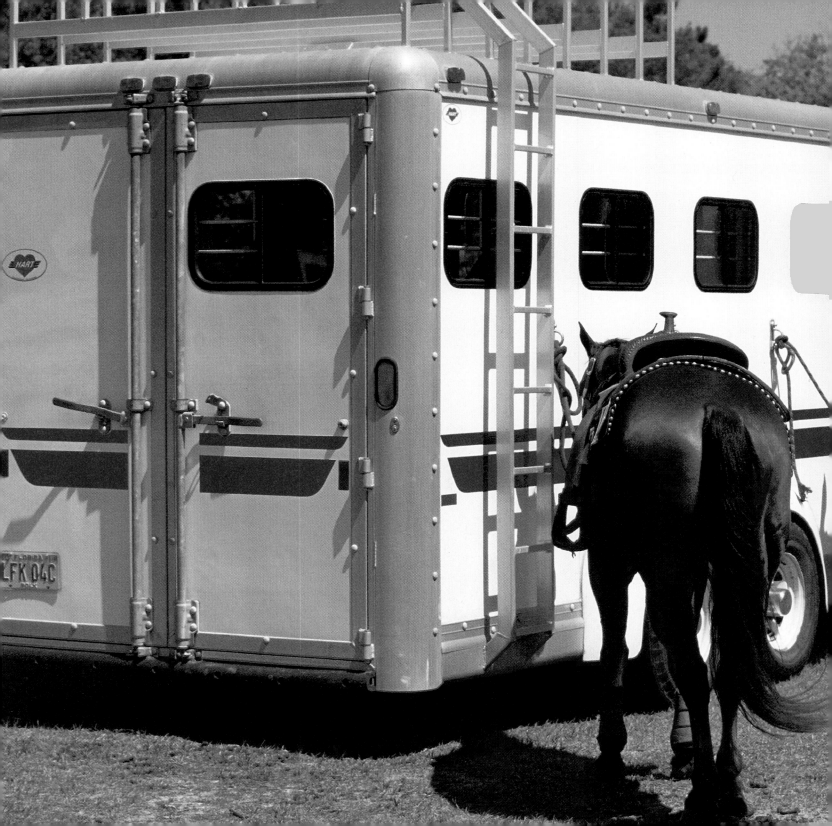

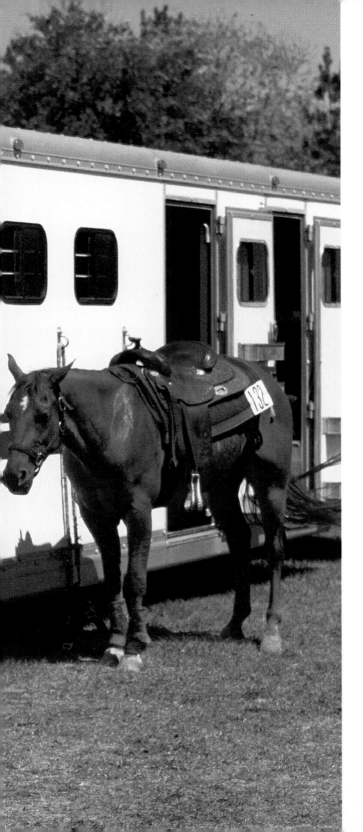

For most Americans, fall is a time of changing leaves, cooling temperatures, and *Monday Night Football*. But those deeply involved with quarter horses may never notice these signs of seasonal change. No, their fall is dominated instead by horse trailers, saddle soap, and the butterflies that exist only within the human stomach. Each year, the American Quarter Horse Association sanctions more than 2,400 breed shows in celebration of "America's Horse"; fall is the culmination. Fall is the time of the "really big shows."

The excitement begins in October with the All-American Quarter Horse Congress, held each year in Columbus, Ohio, and sponsored by the Ohio Quarter Horse Association. Billed as the largest horse show in the world dedi-

cated to a single breed, this twenty-day event hosts more than eight thousand horses who compete in almost two hundred events for $2 million in prizes. Half a million spectators or more pack the stands and crowd the aisles to catch glimpses of this American treasure in action. Reveling in the sweet scent of horse, spectators may view the objects of their affections participating in all manner of equine endeavor, including some classes they might not see at other large breed shows such as calf roping, cutting, barrel racing, and freestyle reining.

Freestyle reining is attracting more and more attention these days. It invites horses—typically horses classically trained in traditional reining—to perform to music reining routines created by their riders, who may themselves perform in costume. To witness such an event is to witness pure enjoyment on the part of the riders and the horses, both of whom obviously appreciate the change of pace freestyle reining offers from more traditional competitive fare. Spectators, too, are inevitably struck by the phenomenal athleticism of the horses, as well as the joint creativity and pizzazz inherent within every spin and rollback.

The last trailer's exit from the Congress grounds marks the pending onset of the next big event. After a couple days' breather, it's on to the American Quarter Horse Association World Championship Show held every year in November in Oklahoma City, Oklahoma. Enthusiasts converge on the city from almost all fifty states and a virtual atlas of countries, including Canada, England, Germany, Spain, Venezuela, Japan, France, Italy, and Mexico. With high hopes they enter their talented quarter horses in eighty-six classes, covering the gamut of English, western, and driving disciplines.

Amid the commotion of impatient whinnies, trailer dust, and incessant grooming that collectively mark the true opening ceremony for such an event, competitors review their entries and commit to memory the starting times for each class. While tending to the demanding preparatory details of grooming, organizing, and muscle stretching, all hear the tiny voice in the back of their minds: who will be this year's Superhorse? Designed to honor the profound versatility of the breed, the Superhorse Award is bestowed upon that horse at the World Championships who earns the highest number of points in a minimum of three events in at least two of six categories. These categories address all disciplines in which quarter horses participate, including halter, reining, working cow horse events, jumping, western pleasure, barrel racing, trail, cutting, and pleasure driving.

Age is no barrier to the Superhorse title. Politics play no role. Even the youngest competitors cannot help but dream. *Could it be that my horse will be the next Rugged Lark*, wonders one such rider as she brushes her equine partner during those first hopeful, giddy hours of the World Championships when anything and everything seems possible.

Rugged Lark, a multitalented quarter horse skilled in reining, hunt seat, trail, driving, and dressage, reaped Superhorse honors twice, first in 1985 and again in 1987. After garnering such glory, he toured the country performing a popular bridleless freestyle reining/dressage routine known to bring audiences to their feet, and he served as the U.S. Equestrian Team's official ambassador to the 1996 Olympic Games. Thus this lovely, levelheaded bay symbol of almost supernatural quarter horse versatility naturally inspires quarter horse exhibitors, young and old alike, to aspire to the example he has set for his kind.

While all cannot be Rugged Lark, the dream still serves to inspire. Witness that inspiration as it guides each owner and trainer to urge a horse on to victory. Witness that inspiration in the World Championship halter classes, where horses are judged on how closely they match the classic quarter horse physique. Witness it in the jumping classes where quarter horses prove to the minions gathered to watch them that this breed is just as fluent in English as it is in western. And witness it in those traditional, ever-popular classes inspired by ranch work, where legendary quarter horse cow sense is a prerequisite for entry. At the World Championships—indeed at any show where quarter horses are in attendance, and at any barn or on any trail a quarter horse calls home—every quarter horse is a "Superhorse."

A Mirror to America's Soul

A theory. Had there been no quarter horse created almost four hundred years ago on American soil, had there been no melding of the bloodlines of both English and Spanish horses in the early days of America's history, there would have been no cowboys—or at least cowboys as we have come to know them. No small felt cowboy hats and pint-size boots. No John Wayne cowboy flicks. No anthems to cowboys as heroes.

When we take stock of the contemporary quarter horse and the pervasiveness of her image, the mere thought of a world devoid of the muscular build of this animal and the kind wisdom within her soft, knowing eyes is preposterous. Simply put, the quarter horse's existence, perhaps like America's existence itself, was preordained. Though she had no

A MIRROR TO AMERICA'S SOUL

Chapter Six

official name until the middle of the twentieth century, the quarter horse has been recognized, cherished, and preserved for almost four hundred years—just as was dictated by the grand plan that has for millennia guided the events of human history.

The quarter horse's story is America's story. Wherever and whenever Americans have sought to build the foundation of a unique cultural identity—from the native peoples of the deep south; to those Europeans who sought settlement of colonial America; to pioneer forays into the unknown, often hostile, territory to the west—the quarter horse has been at the heart of every new stride Americans have ventured to take.

Throughout American history, the independent, progressive, though sometimes sadly misguided spirits who have called this nation home have had the foresight to recognize and embrace the quarter horse as a precious resource. In this horse, we see where we have been, where we are going, and where we would like to be. In turn, the quarter horse, an American original, has become a symbol of both America and her worldwide influence, a product of the American melting pot that represents just how resilient, how dynamic and ingenious is the American ideal.

A MIRROR TO America's Soul

Glossary

cannon: the long lower bone on a horse's leg

conformation: the form or shape of a horse's body

cutting: a western event during which a horse and rider have 2 minutes to separate an individual calf or cow from the rest of its herd and keep it in the middle of the pen

dam: the mother of a horse

dressage: a form of exhibition riding in which the horse receives nearly invisible cues from the rider and performs a series of difficult steps and gaits with lightness of step and perfect balance. Dressage also is a classical training method that teaches the horse to be responsive, attentive, willing, and relaxed for the purpose of becoming a better equine athlete.

filly: a female horse under the age of four years, unless she is bred earlier

foal: a horse of either sex aged one year or under

halter class: a show class in which unsaddled horses are led in a halter to be judged for conformation and condition

hand: a standard of equine height measurement derived from the width of a human hand. Each hand equals 4 inches, with fractions expressed in inches. A horse who is 16.2 hands is 16 hands, 2 inches, or 66 inches tall at the withers.

hunt seat: A style of English riding, suited for horses who are hunters and jumpers, based on traditions in the hunt field. In a variety of show classes, hunters are judged on style and manners as they go over jumps, while jumpers are judged on their ability to get over tough obstacles without knocking them down.

oxer: a jump made of two separate elements of a fence that are jumped as one

pedigree: the recorded list of a horse's ancestors

reining: A western event with origins in ranch work, a reining horse and rider perform a set pattern of movements and gaits, including sliding stops, spins, and rollbacks